Caring for Nigel

Diary of a Wife Coping With Her Husband's Dementia

Eileen Murray

ISBN: 978-1-8383617-2-3

CONTENTS

FOREWORD

At the age of sixty-nine my uncle, Nigel Murray, was diagnosed with dementia. Doctors suspected he was suffering with a rare and degenerative neurological disorder known as Multiple System Atrophy (MSA) involving loss of brain and spinal cord cells. However, Nigel also had many of the symptoms of both Parkinson's disease and Lewy Body dementia and an official diagnosis was never made. Alongside the dementia, were other troubling symptoms: sleep apnoea, rigidity of movement, incontinence, dizziness, slow speech, double vision, nausea and hallucinations.

For four years Nigel's wife, Eileen, kept a diary. This became her "safety valve" - an outlet for the daily stresses of caring for Nigel at home as his mental and physical health slowly deteriorated. In it she gives a frank and detailed account of the endless disturbed nights, his challenging and erratic behaviour, and the relentless struggle with his incontinence. The diary also charts her quest to find respite care, and her mixed feelings when Nigel is finally moved to a full-time residential home.

In his day, Nigel was a well-respected and hard-working university lecturer. Before this, he spent a number of years as an officer in the Army. I remember Nigel as an extremely kind and gentle man and a devoted husband and father. Nigel and Eileen were married in Scotland in 1967. Their son, daughter and grandchildren live in England.

In 2007, Eileen showed me her handwritten diary. I found it a compelling read: very sad and touching, but with her usual dry Scottish wit shining through. With over 25 years' experience as a nurse, Eileen made a very capable and efficient carer. I was shocked, as were the rest of the family, to discover the extent of the ordeal that she had been privately enduring.

I offered to transcribe Eileen's diary, as I felt it could be helpful to others going through a similar experience. After typing it up and circulating a few copies to close family, I filed it away and forgot all about it. In 2013 I stumbled across it again and felt an urge to have it finally published. Here it is.

All names have been changed.

Sophia Ferguson
Eileen & Nigel's Niece

2002: CARING AT HOME

8 MAY 2002

It is distressing for me to write this but I feel that recent events in our lives should be committed to paper - a safety valve for me.

My husband, Nigel, was diagnosed about two years ago with dementia. Doctors suspect he may have Multiple System Atrophy (MSA), a disease almost unknown to most people, including the medical profession. (A definite diagnosis can only be made on autopsy). The disease is progressive and incurable and is very similar to Parkinson's disease in many ways: a mask-like expression, rigidity of movement in the limbs, slow speech, incontinence and constipation.

In addition to the typical Parkinson's symptoms, there are a variety of other symptoms which probably fit into the MSA category: nausea, digestive disturbances, double vision, hallucinations and postural hypotension (dizziness on standing

3

up). These were present to a small degree before medication, which consists of increasing doses of Sinemet (L-dopa) since December 2001.

Nigel has two hip replacements which are successful and trouble free. After the two operations, about five and ten years ago respectively, he hallucinated badly and behaved in a bizarre fashion in the hospital ward. Parkinson's patients do not tolerate narcotic drugs. I suspected for a long time that he had a Parkinson's-like problem and mentioned it to various people who disagreed. Having worked for 25 years in hospitals as a nurse, I was familiar with the movement patterns of these patients.

As the Sinemet pills are increased, Nigel's general mobility has improved and he is able to go for short walks, usually with company, and can climb stairs and get in and out of bed with minimal help. His night incontinence (we put off the lights at about 12am-1am for the night), is managed by pads supplied by the incontinence nurse. The daytime bladder problems are different in that control is partially intact and only light pads are needed, more for confidence than real necessity.

Breakfast's Ready

Today, the usual pattern of getting up and bathing was disrupted more than usual by awful hallucinations and refusal to comply with the routine. Nigel usually has a bath every morning to clean up after a wet night. To help him into the bath, the occupational therapist has provided a pneumatic bath aid called a "Mangar Booster". This is a bath lift which assists transfer to and from the bath. Nigel can't fathom how to use it, despite having daily instructions over a period of a year or so.

Today, Nigel refused to get into the bath and slammed the bathroom door shut. When I managed to gain entry, the bathroom floor was covered with clean incontinence pads (about seven) and Nigel said he had to do an urgent plumbing job and I should call Mr King, the plumber. As I could see nothing wrong, I cleared away the pads and started again to urge him to have a bath. Nigel slammed the bathroom door again, this time locking me out. I wondered what the hell to do.

After some time wondering whether I should break the lock, I decided to appeal to his stomach. I knocked on the door and said "breakfast's ready" and hoped for a response. The door opened and I found he had climbed into the end of the bath without lowering the booster seat and had somehow managed to clamber out - a most dangerous operation. He thought the house was full of people and I had to divert him into dressing. His bottom was bleeding, so I had to sponge the scratched area. After dressing, we went downstairs for breakfast which was uneventful - thank god!

Hallucinations

Nigel is talking more now about his hallucinations, as I think he felt embarrassed to talk about this bewildering subject before. Sometimes I am duplicated or triplicated, being either two wives or a mother and daughter and wife, all residing in different parts of the house with a transient, almost phantom-like, presence. I can often be in two places at once. For instance, while breakfasting, he might remark that there is a scruffy looking woman upstairs cleaning out the bath. It's me! At other times, he welcomes some presence into the room and often this invisible person is offered a seat. This lasts a very short time, as I usually say I can't see anyone and he realises there is no one there.

Every morning on waking I am regaled with the most amazing rubbish-talk. If I relate this back to Nigel later in the day, I will be told it is a dream and he doesn't think he was properly awake when he said it. This morning he said he must get busy as he had to make an analysis of all the British airports. Sometimes he whispers in case some unseen being in the house will find out where private documents are kept. The house, although empty, seems to be pretty heavily populated according to Nigel.

By lunchtime, he is almost himself, in a very modified fashion (having been quite dynamic before the illness), and I can direct him to a comfy chair and escape to the shops, the golf course, or to see friends. The routine is relentless and if changed too much, causes an awful muddle for him.

9 MAY 2002

Main Problems Are In The Morning

I had a chat with Nigel about his early morning behaviour and how it was a bit alarming for me. He showed great sadness, saying the last thing he wanted was to upset our good relationship. The chat bore fruit and the next morning he was very helpful and didn't shut me out of the bathroom. I had already had a disturbed night, as he had taken off his apnoea mask at 3.30am and awoke me because he couldn't remember which button to press to prevent the air puffing out. Then again at 7am, he awoke me to ask me how to go to the loo with a large night pad on. He usually disturbs me about five out of seven nights.

Eventually, I had a downstairs bath at 8.15am (we have an upstairs and downstairs bathroom) and then I rushed up to run his bath, lay out and tape incontinence pads into his underpants, put itch cream on his bottom, wash his hair, scrub his back and, if necessary, cut his toe and fingernails. He manages to dress about three quarters of himself, but can't figure out which leg to put into his underpants and into which slot - an activity that should be solidly embedded after so many years practice.

Breakfast is at about 9.30am and consists of various cereals and bran, with a fruit juice drink or milk, which I lay out with his first dose of Sinemet. As his blood pressure drops, he tends to feel a bit faint and cradles his head in his hands and looks miserable. He leaves the breakfast room and finds a comfortable armchair, and I get on with cleaning up and doing the laundry. He wears a clean shirt, underpants, socks and pyjamas every day, and there are often sheets to wash when he misses getting up in time.

The Apnoea Machine

Nigel experiences sleep apnoea at night which involves frequent pauses in his breathing during sleep. A sleep apnoea machine is needed at night to help with breathing.

The apnoea machine is a frightful nuisance to put on at night. Nigel used to understand the head harness but now he looks at it for ages and puts it on upside-down or sideways. I show him every night and have actually drawn eyes for greater ease but he rarely manages to put it on and if he does, it is more of a fluke than skill.

Nigel has a marked degree of dyspraxia (clumsiness). His speech is also variable in strength and this distresses him as he used to be a lecturer with a loud clear voice. The delivery of speech is hesitant, accompanied by what I would describe, rightly or wrongly, as a marked expressive dysphasia (difficulty stringing his words together), although deafness perhaps blurs interpretation of words. He has a deaf-aid which he doesn't like wearing and only has on occasionally.

16 MAY 2002

A Threatening Gesture

I went downstairs to have a quick bath just after 8am and told Nigel I would be back up to give him a bath in twenty minutes. When I came up, he was in the bathroom telling me that he could manage and didn't want me around. I saw that the bath water was too hot and that the Mangar Booster wasn't plugged in, so I went out to the hall to turn on the switch. On return, I was told not to interfere or he would hit me. I said that this set up wasn't safe and again he said he would hit me and raised his arm in a threatening gesture. He has *never* done anything aggressive before, so I withdrew after quickly putting some cold water into the bath. I saw him climbing into the bath alongside the raised Mangar and trying to sit down. I was afraid to do anything, as I was too shocked by his threatening behaviour.

On returning to the bathroom, I found him squeezed into a very small space in the bath and I was told to remove myself, which I did. About ten minutes later, he shouted from the bathroom and I saw him standing and ready to walk through to the bedroom. I put a towel round him and he walked to the bedroom and he asked me what speed he should go at. He thought 17mph would be about right. I am committing this to paper as it's a safety mechanism for me, because I am completely distressed and fed up.

By lunchtime, the episode did not even register and when I mentioned it to him to find out what was going on in his brain, he was very unhappy at offending the person he loved best in the world. This made me feel rotten for feeling upset earlier but let's face it, I didn't want him to give me a black eye! In the evening, we went out to play bridge with friends and he played quite a reasonable game, and enjoyed the company and food. He was quiet but fairly alert.

We no longer eat out as Nigel's blood pressure drops dramatically after eating. He can collapse and have to lie down and people start fussing about, although he usually recovers in about twenty minutes.

20 MAY 2002

Nigel was very confused in the morning. He said that there was a mark on the front of the wooden lavatory seat called the Mary McPherson mark!

Nigel is also being unhelpful, not intentionally, in his dressing procedure. This morning he pulled the incontinence pads off his underpants, which I had just taped on, and spun a tale about how he no longer needed them.

Most days we go for car runs locally and sometimes have a short walk in the park to watch the swans and the cygnets.

21 MAY 2002

I am looking for accommodation for cousin Bob and his wife, Shirley, as it is too awkward to have them staying here with Nigel's erratic behaviour. I found a Bed & Breakfast round the corner.

28 MAY 2002

A Visit From Bob And Shirley

Nigel was very pleased to see Bob and Shirley and responded well to the chats about the past. We spent time in the local park and Nigel was able to enjoy a walk round. Bob and Shirley were very thoughtful and understanding. Shirley is a physiotherapist and understands the immobility problems and I find it helpful to discuss this with her.

30 MAY 2002

Yellow Socks

Nigel thinks he is taking part in a foot competition tomorrow and must wear yellow socks - his favourites! He is getting more and more lazy about helping himself and finds it difficult to stand up from sitting on the bath seat. He leans heavily on me, which is beginning to take its toll on my back. The Community Alarm System (CAS) is working and Nigel can wear an alarm pendant round his neck, which gives me more confidence to leave him at home.

1 JUNE 2002

Things Are Getting Worse

I got up early to prepare breakfast and give Nigel a bath. We are to attend our friend Joyce's funeral at 11am. When I came upstairs after feeding the cat, I heard water running. To my horror I found Nigel in the bath with all his nightwear floating round him, including a thick jersey he had put on. Worst of all, a huge urine saturated incontinence pad was floating in the water. I fished these objects out with tongs and asked him what he had done. He said it was because the Mangar Booster was not in use. Carol the cleaner had taken the Mangar out of the bath to clean the bath thoroughly. Things are getting worse.

Nigel had no idea what was going on. He said I was giving him too many instructions when I told him not to wash his face in the bath, as the water was dirty.

5 JUNE 2002

Bizarre and Erratic Behaviour

Nigel woke me at 2.30am and wanted to know how to turn off his apnoea machine. That information took about ten minutes. I suppose I could have reached across the bed and pushed the switch, which he couldn't find in spite of turning it on every night, but my back was killing me. I had also entertained all my Scrabble players the night before and was sleepy. I gave him repeated directions, which he eventually understood.

In the morning, I awoke to find Nigel had run and had a bath, negotiating one hazard after another. He then said he would call his mother (dead for years) to secure his incontinence pads into his Y-front underpants. I said that his mother had died and he said perhaps her assistant - me - could help! He dressed himself completely after that and went downstairs. His behaviour is erratic and bizarre.

7 JUNE 2002

A Very Bad Episode

I went downstairs early to have a quick bath while Nigel was asleep. When I came upstairs to the bedroom, I found him having a pee into the wastepaper basket, having done most of it over the carpet and his slippers. I was pretty miffed and told him so. After I had cleaned up the carpet - about 12 foot in length - I said "Don't do that again!" in no uncertain terms, to which he replied "I suspect some other chaps will do it on the carpet now that you've made it clean again". I'm fed up!

I wrote to Dr Morgan about the "bizarre episodes", asking him for his advice on a reduction of pill dosage, enough to reduce the hallucinations but at the same time enough to retain mobility.

10 JUNE 2002

Need a Social Worker

Nigel woke at 6am needing help with incontinence pads and I had to persuade him to put on another one, which he couldn't think how to do himself. Later in the bath, he said he was 56 (he's actually 72) and about to be interviewed for an important new job position. After breakfast he locked the dining room doors because he wished to protect some top secret exam papers - and so it goes on and on and on. After these early episodes, he spends the whole day sitting about doing nothing, in spite of being asked to do a few routine tasks.

11 JUNE 2002

Leg Muscles Weakening

I had a phone call from Dr Morgan in response to my letter sent on 7 June. He says that a reduction of pills probably wouldn't help and that I should wait for Dr Patel's hospital assessment of his condition and type of dementia and perhaps drugs could be prescribed to improve things.

Nigel is very lethargic today. I gave him a bath with the Mangar Booster as I didn't feel it was safe to allow him to struggle and perhaps fall. Even with the Mangar, I had a tough pull to get Nigel to standing position. His leg muscles are weakening. Later at about 5.30pm, he put on a dressing gown over his clothes and said he was going downstairs to have a bath. He said he didn't want to use the Mangar as he can't manage it. I was very busy and said that one bath was all I could cope with, with all the dressing and undressing. He is very determined so I had to let him go. My whole day is programmed by his needs and any project I start is quickly disturbed (except golf when he can't reach me). People look in on him, or phone him, while I'm out.

12 JUNE 2002

This morning, when I suggested that Nigel have a bath (I had already had mine downstairs), he said "How much will it cost? Can we afford it?" That was soon resolved and he got into the bath using the Mangar. Uneventful bath!

15 JUNE 2002

Lethargy

Nigel is not very well. He is very lethargic and wanting to lie down and is reluctant to exercise. At breakfast, after a struggle getting him bathed and downstairs, he announced that he had been married several times and might have children I don't know about! This is not true as far as I know. I feel he is sinking into a terminal lethargy like the patients that I used to work with, who would spend all day sleeping or staring into space. It is so sad that such a gifted person should end up like this. The presence of our two children, John and Kate, who came to stay yesterday from London, has brightened him up, but they notice a huge and distressing change.

26 JUNE 2002

How Much Longer Can I Cope?

Nigel's deterioration is very rapid and he can barely follow any sequence of instructions. Even on much repeated tasks, such as washing himself in the bath, he constantly refers to me for instructions on what to do next. He also spends a long time examining his apnoea machine at night and cannot fathom where the top is, or how to put it on. He occasionally manages quite by accident. When I instruct him for the hundredth time, he gets irritable and sometimes tells me to shut up. This behaviour is very marked this morning. His thoughts clear a bit during the day but he is very dependent, constantly asking for cues and then accusing me of being bossy.

I really wonder how long I can cope with such dependency as I, too, am no longer young (68) and although very active, do have aches and pains in my joints. If he is hospitalised, he may be put with really incompatible demented patients and I would feel dreadful. On the other hand, if I persevere with him at home, I can save colossal nursing home fees, money which we could use to help the children. The stock market is collapsing today and that's another possible problem.

27 JUNE 2002

Toffees

I had a very bad start to the day with Nigel getting up and taking off his pads and wandering about the bedroom looking for somewhere to dispose of them. After his bath, I told him to walk to his chair and sit down. He didn't do this and when I remonstrated he said "You're in a mood for killing embryos this morning!" I let him get on with things without intervention.

Later, in the morning post, a postcard arrived from Cornwall with two clotted cream toffee sweets attached. In the evening, I said to Nigel that it would be fun to try them. He couldn't remember where he had put the postcard and eventually told me it was in his dressing table drawer. I fetched the postcard which was there *minus* the sweets. He then remembered that he had eaten both of them when he was "in a dreamlike state". I know it's childish but I felt a bit done out of a tiny treat, particularly as it had come from our son, John, and his wife Claire.

My freedom is retreating and I feel that soon I won't be able to go out anywhere. Already, I am having to make fairly complex plans, with people phoning him at intervals, just so that I can play in the Open Ladies Golf Championship up the road.

30 JUNE 2002

Burglar Alarm

I was woken at 6am by the burglar alarm going off, so got up and switched it off and then realised Nigel wasn't in bed. I found him in the breakfast room fully dressed and having breakfast saying that he had got up too early. He said he had alerted the burglar alarm company that it was a false alarm and that he had spoken to Carol, our cleaner, who apparently was working on the alarm company switchboard - complete fantasy!

I went upstairs and changed his soiled bedding and turned the mattress and did some washing and then I went back to bed. Fed up. When I got up, I gave Nigel a bath and he had no idea what was going on and didn't recognise the Mangar Booster, or how it worked. At his second breakfast, he said there was a soldier in the breakfast room when asked to whom he was speaking. I feel he is almost ready to take up residence somewhere where he can have round-the-clock care as I'm worn out, but the idea appals me.

3 JULY 2002

Bath Flood

Nigel disturbed me at about 3am to say there was a person in black standing in the room by the door. I calmed him down and said it was just his dressing gown hanging on the door. Then he said he couldn't cope with the task of lifting a heavy kettle full of stones. This episode passed after a short time and we both went back to sleep.

At 7am, I woke up and found the apnoea machine disconnected, but still puffing air, and Nigel was not around. As I assumed he had gone to the bathroom I waited for a bit, drifting in and out of sleep. After some time, I found him still missing from the bedroom, so went to the bathroom. He was in a very deep bath which had flooded the complete bathroom floor which is carpeted with tiles. He was enjoying his bath without the Mangar Booster. I went moderately ballistic and pointed out the carpet and then started lifting the very saturated tiles, which dripped everywhere. I then went downstairs to see if the hall ceiling below was still intact. It looked ok.

During this episode, Nigel seemed quite detached and thought I was making a fuss about a trivial matter. I helped him out of the bath and left him to dress as best he could, while I tried to mop up the mess. There were also urine-soaked incontinence pads about the place, and clearing up was unpleasant. Later, water started dripping through the ceiling by the front door.

My first reaction was that I couldn't stand anymore of this behaviour, although I know he can't help it but even so, it drives one mad. I would almost welcome a break if he were to be "sectioned" but would feel very guilty for not waiting until the possible hallucinatory effects of the Sinemet pills were carefully assessed. If he was placed in a good nursing home, I could bring him home often and I might get some sleep. I thought I would have a chat with the occupational therapist or social worker about future plans but after hanging on the phone for ages with no reply, gave up.

7 JULY 2002

Nigel is more amenable today but will use only one special "anti-dandruff" comb. He said he had a special notice from the authorities about the properties of this comb!

11 JULY 2002

Private Documents

Nigel is very confused and thinks that a bath will alter his body shape and that this is controlled by some authority, probably me or my assistant, whoever that might be.

Later at breakfast, he was still confused and arrived with different shoes on and some documents concerning mandates and direct debits stuffed up his jersey. He then summoned me upstairs to have a chat in private about documents, in a place where we would not be overheard. We were the only people in the house. I removed the documents and he soon forgot about them.

16 JULY 2002

Very Deranged

Nigel is very deranged. After an early start at 7.45am for his bath, because I hoped to go for a round of golf, Nigel locked himself in the sitting room. He said he wanted to guard some share cheques which had come by post. Also, he thought the room was doubling as a bathroom.

I eventually persuaded him to open the door and found he had moved his armchair and seemed to think it was a lavatory. He had his underpants down and was in a grumpy mood and was about to defecate in the armchair. He didn't and I persuaded him to go to the bathroom where he sat on the loo without removing his underpants and fortunately didn't perform.

By the evening, he was more lucid but by 11pm was completely confused again and unable to understand how to change an incontinence pad if soiled, in spite of copious demonstrations. It's so hard for both of us to cope with, particularly at 3am or thereabouts, on about five nights out of seven. I am feeling worn out again.

17 JULY 2002

Nigel awoke and told me his mother had died during the night. I told him that she had died about fourteen years ago but he persisted until I made him aware that she had died while playing a game of bridge. He then remembered most of the event.

20 JULY 2002

A Special Remedy

Nigel woke me at 3am, 4am, 5am, 6am and 7am and I drifted off to sleep at 8am. I half realised he was moving about and then he appeared at the bedroom door having given himself a bath using, he said, the Mangar Booster which he really doesn't understand. He said that certain military authorities, including me, had organised all these activities. My back was very sore so I lay in bed. He knows I sometimes have a sore back and he approached me with a special remedy which involved laying a string of pearls by my bedside. Oh dear, what next!

He dressed himself, after a fashion, and disappeared downstairs saying that he would save some cereal for our son, John. John is in London.

22 JULY 2002

Apnoea Tubing

Nigel took off his apnoea tubing during the night and started thrashing the three foot tubing all over the place. I escaped being hit. This nightmare was soon over and I reconnected the tubing to his mask.

I was disturbed again at 5am by the sound of the bath running. I told him to turn it off and come to bed, making sure he was well padded in case of incontinence. I was very fed up and almost lost my temper but he went to bed.

I was again disturbed at 7.30am but by this time I had had enough and went downstairs to have a bath. I came upstairs and ran his bath and bathed him. At this session, he thought I was his mother.

Later, a walk in the park was accomplished without reference to, or probably without memory of, earlier events. I am so tired I nearly fell asleep in the supermarket car park when I went to do my elderly neighbour's shopping.

During the day, Nigel is lethargic but not completely switched off and he spends quite a bit of time doing what looks like mathematical puzzles. He is more alert as the day goes on but unable to deal with bills or tax and legal documents.

26 JULY 2002

Only So Much One Can Take

After a dreadful night of disturbances, taking off the apnoea mask and not turning off the air supply and shouting and snoring, Nigel woke me later than usual at 8.30am wanting to have a bath. My back was very sore, but I managed to heave myself out of bed to find Nigel on the point of peeing onto the edge of the bed. I grabbed a urine bottle and told him to pee into it and he pushed me aside and persisted, so I gently smacked his hand and told him I would leave him if he peed on the bed. I then had to run his bath while he talked awful rubbish.

I later changed all the bedding and turned the mattress which was well protected and unmarked. This was hard as my back was hurting. Then I felt a bit dizzy and guilty that I could smack Nigel when I know he is potty, but there is only so much one can take. He is quite unaware of any conversations at this time of day, thankfully.

31 JULY 2002

Fantasies

I woke after a disturbed night. Nigel had had a bad nightmare and had been waving his arms about. At 7.30am, I found he had got up and was having some sort of bath without the Mangar Booster. I left him to it as my back was locked and I had to move about gingerly to free it up. It is all right once I get moving.

This morning, Nigel thought he had to rush about as he expected four midshipmen on board our ship, HMS Carlton (our house is in Carlton Road). I was to teach them on a course of electrical engineering and Nigel was giving me the rank of Lieutenant - he being a Lieutenant Colonel. I hope he soon forgets all this fantasy as I'm worn out with it.

2 AUGUST 2002

A Trip to the Cash Dispenser

In the afternoon, we walked to the bank and Nigel wanted to use the cash dispenser outside. He completely messed up the procedure and we had a huge, irritated-looking, queue waiting. Eventually, a bank employee reluctantly appeared, as they were closing down, and verified that no cash had been removed from the machine. This is just one of many muddling episodes which happen during the day.

3 AUGUST 2002

Banking Issues

At 9am, Nigel decided that the temperature in his bath was changing from cold to hot all the time and he was very anxious to get out in case he was either frozen or boiled. The bath was a comfortable temperature, which he normally enjoys, and no additional water had been added. It may be a bad day ahead.

Later, Nigel refuses to find out our bank balance. I wanted to know after his banking episode yesterday during which the bank employee said she wanted to discuss options as, to her mind, we had too big a balance. I said it was safer than the stock market. I now want to know where our bank statements are, which Nigel normally keeps meticulous care of in his office. I have never been encouraged to know about bank affairs. It appears we have four bank accounts and Nigel has put off explaining how the system works. He explained a little last year, which I wrote down, but not enough to have immediate access. I have Power of Attorney but can't use it if I don't know how to organise this money.

4 AUGUST 2002

Today, Nigel is hallucinating and talking rubbish. He thought he was going to a funeral.

5 AUGUST 2002

Slacking

Nigel woke up and said his hands were not working and he would need some special exercises. I told him to clap his hands, which helped, and although I could see no change in his hand mobility from yesterday, it persisted until I gave him a bath. In the bath, he was annoyed that I had dashed downstairs to sort out breakfast and feed the cat, and said the system would have to be revised as it didn't suit him waiting in the bath. He had climbed out of the bath not using the Mangar Booster and was quite annoyed with me for slacking! And so it goes on. (P.S. I have lost half a stone slacking!) He has been muddled, as well as faint, after meals and was talking rubbish.

12 AUGUST 2002

The Memory Clinic

In the bath, when asked how he was getting on, Nigel said that the petrol station had given him six minutes and after that he would be going on to nuclear fuel!

Last week we visited the Memory Clinic and saw Dr Park, a physician, who took a case history and advised us that memory pills, the type given for Alzheimer's, were unsuitable as the side effects would probably amplify already troublesome symptoms such as muscle rigidity, nausea and incontinence. He suggested that a visit from a psychiatric nurse, or similar, might be useful in advising on management, and perhaps this would give me some relief.

Dr Park said that confusion was part of the Parkinson's spectrum and would probably not respond to medication. We did not see Dr Patel as expected. The Memory Clinic is mainly concerned with Alzheimer's patients.

23 AUGUST 2002

Five Disturbances in the Night

Things have been fairly peaceful up until today. Last night there were five disturbances and I had to clean up a puddle in the bathroom at 3.30am. In the morning I was too tired to give him a bath and he made a fuss about washing at the basin. I felt my energy ebbing but there was no choice but to get on with things.

The most irritating aspect of the morning sessions is the almost uninterruptible flow of rubbish conversation and preoccupation with self. If I say I am tired, he says he is *very* tired, and he probably does feel awful. Today, I feel he needs a nursing home for night care.

7 SEPTEMBER 2002

Thinks He's the Pope!

It is so routine for Nigel to be hallucinating in the morning, I rather expect it and, although upsetting, have tried to switch off from the distress that I used to experience. Today he thought he was the Pope!

Lewy Body Dementia

At 11.30am, we went to see a neurologist at the local hospital. He said that Nigel has some of the symptoms associated with Lewy Body dementia. Apparently, MSA and Lewy Body dementia often share certain features. He said he could offer no further treatment, apart from Sinemet. So now we have to go it alone. He said we didn't need to come back but could if Nigel wanted. Nigel didn't take in much of the interview, which was a blessing as there was no cheer in it but I did feel we should keep in touch. His deafness and problem with words didn't help and nor did the time of day.

Dr Park, the Memory Clinic physician who tested him last month, had written to Dr Davidson advising against dementia drugs as they would not be beneficial, he felt. A depressing morning.

9 SEPTEMBER 2002

Trousers With the "Appetite Mechanism"

Nigel asked for his trousers with the "appetite mechanism" when he was dressing! Quite funny. He must want to eat a lot today.

His general disposition over the last few months has been lethargy but friends say he responds well to their telephone chats. He still has a lot of social faculties intact but he can't take new concepts on board.

10 SEPTEMBER 2002

Deep Inward Distress

A bad night. Nigel woke me at 4am and said we were on a motoring trip and that he had dropped a pen from the car and would I go and fetch it. My reactions are not printable. Later, he was very reluctant to have a bath in spite of the fact that he had scratched his bottom raw and was bleeding. I insisted. He thought he had won the "old crocks" race and a bath was irrelevant. I was told not to give so many instructions about how to get into the bath and he was really very autocratic and difficult. I am fed up but as he can't help it, I have no response except deep inward distress.

17 SEPTEMBER 2002

Fault on the Telephone Line

Nigel's alertness is variable and he played a reasonable, if slow, game of bridge. He had a bad nightmare which was rather disturbing and was jumping about the bed.

At lunch time he picked a piece of herb (Rosemary) out of the soup and said it might be responsible for the fault on the telephone line. An engineer is coming to fix the fault later on today. I told Nigel not to mention it to the engineer. I hope he won't!

24 SEPTEMBER 2002

Visit to the Dementia Geriatric Clinic

Dr Hammond chatted for some time, listening to all the symptoms and also to my ability, or non-ability, to cope with the ever worsening dementia. He suggested a mild sleeping pill to counteract Nigel's nightmares and said Nigel had a condition where the REM sleep was not detaching the thoughts from the actions - hence the night time activity. It might help me too if he sleeps better.

Dr Hammond also suggested a respite home up north where we could both go and be cared for on holiday. The idea doesn't appeal to me as I thought he would be going alone and I could have a break in London to see family. The doctor will send brochures. Dr Hammond was very helpful and considerate and we are to return later in the year. He said the sleeping pills would not interfere with the Sinemet.

6 OCTOBER 2002

Feeling Lousy

The brochure for the holiday home arrived today and it is a series of purpose-built, ground floor, self-contained units with kitchen, bedroom, bathroom and appliances. The place caters for the blind, wheelchair bound and others. It has a large communal conservatory with a giant TV. All supplies have to be brought, and other necessities can be bought locally. The whole scenario does not appeal and I don't want to take Nigel somewhere that sounds pretty basic and where I have to cook. It doesn't sound like a rest.

Our lawyer, Anne McDonald, has just phoned to say she has had several identical phone calls from Nigel about some shares. He quite forgets he has made them and Anne is going spare about the whole issue.

I have a dreadful cold and throat infection and Nigel, although concerned, can't help. When I asked if I could have a long lie in the morning (i.e. another 20 minutes) as I felt lousy, he said "Don't worry, I'll get the staff downstairs to attend to everything". If I have a "bad" illness, he will have to be admitted somewhere. Our son, John, is at home for a few days and very helpful.

8 OCTOBER 2002

Cotton Polo Necks

Not such a good night with Nigel having difficulty turning. He is obviously uncomfortable but kept his apnoea machine on most of the night. In the morning, he was ok in the bath but later arrived at breakfast having got himself out of the bath and got his dressing muddled while I was downstairs.

He arrived at breakfast without a shirt and with a fairly itchy jersey on. I suggested that he put a shirt on, which did not appeal to him, so I think I will put him into cotton polo necks for casual wear, if he will co-operate. Generally, he needs nearly everything either suggested, prompted, or done for him.

Last night my Scrabble friends were here and Nigel joined in the chat but not to play. They said I needed a break and wondered how long I could cope with the constant care. I am so busy that I don't have too much time to consider my lot, and it's not as bad as some people have.

I wish I could love Nigel as I used to but he is so changed and indifferent to my tiredness that I keep having to remind myself that he's been a kind husband in the past and that he can't help the present. If he dies, I shall feel both relieved and devastated, and guilty that I couldn't spend more time listening to, and trying to make sense of, his ramblings.

12 OCTOBER 2002

Awful Muddles Around Early Morning

After a late night out playing bridge with friends, which Nigel managed to do after a fashion, Nigel went to sleep quite quickly after taking the sleeping pill. In the morning, I found him in half the bath, the Mangar Booster unused at the other half, and Nigel squeezed in a very awkward position. I managed to extricate him by letting the air out of the Mangar and lifting it out - a great weight. Later in the day, he had no recollection of the incident.

His appetite has increased and he is always looking around for food, although he has an ample diet. All day long he loses things and asks odd questions and hallucinates.

23 OCTOBER 2002

Forever Mopping

Nigel has increasing lapses in behaviour and an endless stream of bizarre ideas and hallucinations. He is able to do very little for himself. Occasionally, he asserts his authority and tries to cope with the ever increasing backlog of documents but achieves very little and muddles my ability to cope.

After a visit to Dr Green, I am allowed to give Nigel a sleeping pill when I think it is appropriate, rather than every night. For the last two days, I have given him half a pill so as to withdraw gently.

Nigel's behaviour is erratic and he keeps taking off his incontinence night pads and creating a lot of work for me. Also, he goes to the lavatory in the middle of the night and performs anywhere adjacent to the lav - on his slippers, the floor, or the carpet - and I'm forever mopping. I had to change his pads at 5.30am and after a rotten night's sleep I feel exhausted.

We visited the apnoea clinic and got a new face piece.

25 OCTOBER 2002

In the morning at bath time, Nigel said that we should each have two friends in either Scotland or England. I didn't wait for him to enlarge on this topic. He is still muddled but not as muddled as when he's taken his sleeping pill. I think we're both exhausted.

26 OCTOBER 2002

Power of Attorney

I cancelled Nigel's bridge game with his three university colleagues because he is so switched off and has to have the bidding repeated all the time, and then immediately forgets or gets it wrong. The bridge coincided with one of the three having a bad cold, so he was glad to cancel.

Nigel's daily behaviour is very wearing for me and sad for him, although he seems unable to grasp the oddness of his actions. For example, he took his trousers half down in the sitting room this morning and thought he might have wet something. I examined the chairs and floor to find he hadn't had an accident at all but ushered him to the lav, where he complied.

Another problem is taking his pills which I dole out. He sometimes mixes them into his cornflakes into which he's already emptied his "fybogel" laxative.

Every daily activity has to be prompted: bathing, dressing, shaving, eating, getting to bed and putting on incontinence night pads and apnoea mask, which I usually have to do. He can be very obstructive.

My brother, Angus, who is a retired solicitor, is trying to alleviate future problems by drawing up an updated version of the Power of Attorney (the old one is out of date). This will come into action if Nigel becomes incapable, without having to revert to a Curator appointed by the Court, and will help me sort out things if Nigel deteriorates. This new one will have to be signed by a doctor and a solicitor, giving more power to me.

30 OCTOBER 2002

Trying Not to Lose My Temper

At 8.30am I awoke to find Nigel had taken off all his nightwear and pads and was talking about "brackets from India". I couldn't understand a word. I told him that if he took his pads off I would have a huge amount of work to do, but he went on talking about brackets.

I got up and ran his bath and while I was in the bathroom preparing for him, he arrived naked leaving a trail of urine from bed to bathroom - about 25 feet. I had to get down on my knees and disinfect and mop up. I am trying hard not to lose my rag and understand that dementia ruins his *and* my life.

6 NOVEMBER 2002

I phoned the social work department and was put on a social worker list. They will call sometime. At last!

7 NOVEMBER 2002

A Very Worrying Morning

I found Nigel in the sitting room with his underpants down trying to defecate on my chair. He was very confused and I was pretty sharp and escorted him upstairs to the bathroom. I told him that he must try and perform in the appropriate place. I said it was very hard for me to cope and apologised for being sharp. He said that it was worse for him finding himself in such a predicament and apologies didn't help. I don't know what to do!

He may need institutionalisation soon but I can't bear the thought one minute and would welcome it the next. The family are due home next week. How will they cope with incidents like this? I phoned the Alzheimer's Society and they are sending a help pack.

9 NOVEMBER 2002

Nigel Weighs 11 Stone 9lbs

After a fairly heavy Ladies Golf Club dinner, Nigel woke me at 5am and asked if I'd like to play chess. I gave a negative response and at 7am the same request came, so I'm tired today. The dementia is increasing daily and I can scarcely go out without making quite sure he is in a reasonable state. When I come back from shopping, he asks me if I have been out golfing, although I have told him repeatedly where I'm off to and very often leave a note.

14 NOVEMBER 2002

A very disturbed night with the apnoea machine and then full pad and pyjama change at 5am. I have earache, which doesn't help, and feel tired.

15 NOVEMBER 2002

Sometimes Nigel says something demented but funny. This morning in the bath he said that in order to "sweeten his anus" he was putting in a pot plant. Sounds a bit of an ordeal!

16 NOVEMBER 2002

Active nightmare - shaking his hands about.

17 NOVEMBER 2002

The Family Visits

I told Nigel that I had to collect Kate (our daughter) from the airport at 7am. He said he must guard the bathroom door from other people so that Kate could have a bath, and was all for standing outside the door. I tried to reassure him that he and I were the only occupants of the house, apart from Kate. It took some persuasion and then he went to sleep. Very wet bed and lots of laundry to do.

Later in the day, I returned from shopping and found he had missed the loo and performed on his clothing. Oh dear, I am a bit tired again especially with Kate, John and his wife, Claire, all visiting. It is lovely seeing them.

Nigel can do very little, although he is quite mobile. He finds it almost impossible to take on board more than one instruction at a time (apraxia). His hands are always ice-cold and blue due to circulatory problems. His appetite is very good though.

22 NOVEMBER 2002

A dreadful day with Nigel's desperate constipation. I thought he would die of the condition, so I got him up and marched him about and the event happened.

30 NOVEMBER 2002

Cyril Is Run Over

Our darling cat, Cyril, has been run over and killed. Nigel and I are devastated.

This morning Nigel said, while bathing, that there was an influx of refugees coming and we must leave Scotland! He is very confused but it improves a bit as the day goes on. It's difficult coping with the memory of our lovely 15 year old cat and being bombarded with demented remarks by Nigel. A friend said on the phone last week that Nigel seemed on the ball and that I was exaggerating his confusion. I said she ought to join us in the morning and after meals and she'd believe me!

Yesterday, I wrote to Dr Hammond enclosing the Council Tax rebate form, which Nigel's Community Nurse had given us, with possible entitlement rebate. Unfortunately, it has a heading "Severe Mental Impairment" and I don't want Nigel to see it as he doesn't think there's much wrong with him.

At the moment, I wash, dress, give baths, make meals and drive him about to masses of doctor's appointments, cope with incontinence and washing, and direct him in most of his activities. He couldn't look after himself and is unable to sort out his pill regime and apnoea appliances.

2 DECEMBER 2002

A phone call from Dr Hammond - he will forward the form to the Council Tax Office.

3 DECEMBER 2002

A message from Nigel having a bath: he said integer variables on the hill were affecting share dividends!

6 DECEMBER 2002

A Can of Beer

After lunch I went out shopping, leaving Nigel with Carol, the cleaner. When I came back she said he had gone out without a coat across to the tennis club opposite the house. When I asked him what he'd been doing, he said he wanted to ask passers-by if they could sell him a can of beer but he didn't meet anyone - thankfully! He hasn't drunk beer for years. Carol has not seen him acting oddly before and was a bit anxious.

18 DECEMBER 2002

Still No Social Worker

For several weeks now, Nigel's behaviour has been becoming more bizarre and difficult to deal with. I feel that I need a break. I broached the subject with Nigel during a lucid interval and he said he would be agreeable to giving me a short break to rest a bit.

I am still waiting to hear from a social worker to help plan long term care, as I feel that if I have a health problem, Nigel's welfare will be an acute, and unplanned for, problem. One of my neighbours is a social worker. She has contacted a senior social worker at the social work department who said she would give me a priority phone call, but nothing has happened. When I phone, I get put on hold or told to try another time. I have been phoning for months.

Nigel's behaviour is disturbing. Today he thought I was his mother. Another time, he knew I was his wife but couldn't remember my name and insisted on calling me Allison! He wanders about the house a lot and this evening he decided to sit on the floor in front of the electric fire. I looked up from where I was working on the computer to see him falling over and leaning against the fire. I remonstrated with him and told him he would burn. He was quite unaware of the danger and I had quite a tug of war putting him into a safe position. Now my back is aching. How long can I go on? I'm extremely busy preparing for Christmas and the family arriving.

Last night, he took all his nightwear off in the middle of the night when I was asleep. I don't know how I managed to sleep through it. Exhaustion!

20 DECEMBER 2002

Nigel is becoming progressively confused and difficult to cope with. Sometimes I feel I'm going mad as he doesn't understand simple instructions and becomes obsessed with things.

I have the brochures for the Eastfield Care Home. I had a look at the outside of the place and saw an old man with a zimmer frame and carpet slippers walking down the drive - rather depressing. I don't think I could cope with leaving Nigel at the door and going home to a lonely house.

Caring for Nigel

2003: SEEKING RESPITE

5 JANUARY 2003

Worrying About the Future

Nigel is progressively more confused, hallucinatory, and disorientated in time and place. Every day is an awful struggle physically and mentally as the dementia progresses.

Nights are becoming more disturbed as Nigel wakes at about 3am and wants to use the loo but can't manage. He can't manage a urine bottle and can't cope with incontinence pads, so I have to get up and change his pads if he is wet. Last night I had to change his pyjama jacket and woolly jersey as well. It took about three quarters of an hour and I couldn't get to sleep as I worry so much about the future and how to cope.

My main worries are Nigel's physical and mental deterioration and the enormous amount of financial affairs to cope with. My friend, Christine, is helping to teach me about PEPs and ISAs and the stock market, as Nigel talks about them but his concentration fades and he can only occasionally find a relevant file. There are about forty files and a large cabinet of financial affairs and lots of loose documents.

Our lawyers send in huge bills each year for managing an amount quite out of proportion to the amount charged, but they are a large reputable firm and they handle all our stocks and shares and our wills. Angus, my brother, helps with our affairs too and I try not to contact the lawyers as we get charged for every letter.

Dr Green phoned today as Nigel collapsed on the floor yesterday and I called an ambulance, which I then cancelled. I called the doctor instead, as Nigel rallied and got up with help. A doctor came and she tested Nigel with neurological tests and took blood and urine specimens for bacteriology.

Dr Green is phoning up the social work department to hasten an assessment, as I need it to further the set-up of respite or long term care for which I need financial advice.

All forms concerning admission to hospitals or homes require the social worker, unless one is going to pay the whole lot privately. Medical and personal care, as legislated in Scotland, can save you up to £210 on weekly fees.

20 JANUARY 2003

Desperate For An Assessment

A very worrying and exhausting day which included Nigel having a bath, prepared and given by me, followed by dressing him almost wholly and then breakfast. He then retired to the bathroom and shut himself in. I waited until he was out, and then put him to lie on his bed and nipped out to do the shopping for our neighbours and us. When I came back, he was still in bed but disorientated.

At lunch, Nigel refused to come to the table and was talking awful rubbish. I eventually sat him down with a mug of soup. After lunch, he disappeared upstairs and I heard the bath running and found he had taken off his clothes and was about to have another bath. He couldn't remember the first bath. I told him that it was unnecessary but he locked the door and somehow managed to fill the bath and have some kind of wash. He wouldn't open the door.

After lunch, Nigel set off to "check the corridors" and also to speak to his stepfather who died long ago. He also had put on a clean shirt and no underpants, so that had to be fixed because of his increasing incontinence.

I phoned up the social work department and got the duty social worker and told her I was desperate for an assessment for residential respite care and couldn't cope with 24-hour disturbance. I didn't tell her that I had been crying with frustration and fatigue.

Marriage is for better or worse and I feel I have to cope whatever, but surely dementia of this kind lets you off the hook a bit. A nursing home might be better for both of us. Financially it is a huge outlay but I would willingly live in a tent just to have some peace.

25 JANUARY 2003

Nightmare of a Day

Nigel wouldn't have his bath in the usual way and nearly fell and took all sorts of risks. When I told him what to do for safety he said "Shut up or I'll bash your face in". I was very upset and everything after that went wrong.

In the afternoon, he went to rest and I went out just to get a breather and shop. When I came home, I just didn't want to speak to him, partly because I'm feeling pretty lousy after poor sleep last night and partly because I couldn't stand the situation.

I would finish myself off if it wasn't for the children. Nigel can't help being like he is, which makes my attitude difficult to live with. He is very very hallucinatory.

1 FEBRUARY 2003

Nigel didn't recognise me this evening and I find this too sad for both of us. I cried with frustration and sadness. It's no good explaining anything as he just can't take it in and he thinks the house is full of people and I could be any of them. He seems obsessed with a lecturer whom he thinks is in the house, and he thinks he must help organise computers for students. Tonight he thought I was his tutor.

I still have had no word from the social work department, as promised. Dr Green has sent the respite application for the Eastfield Care Home and I need a named social worker to advise me. It's awfully expensive having care and I may have to sell the house.

5 FEBRUARY 2003

A Social Worker At Last

Nigel activated the burglar alarm at about 5am. I awoke to find him wandering around and the alarm company phoning but I couldn't get to the phone in time. Then Nigel needed his pad changed. In the middle of this, a detective inspector arrived at the door about the alarm and I had to be interviewed by him and tell him it was a mistake. When I tried later to ring the alarm company, I got the wrong number but it was all eventually sorted out.

I now have a named social worker, Sheena McNab.

11 FEBRUARY 2003

Visit From the Social Worker

I had a helpful visit from Sheena McNab, the social worker, today. She will start respite and possibly a sitting service. I will take Nigel to see three different respite care homes which

Sheena recommends. She will assess our financial input and top up the free personal care and nursing charges. I shall try to find out about our finances and try to get Nigel to fill in various gaps. He occasionally has glimmers of his past abilities, so I must be alert to these moments.

18 FEBRUARY 2003

Very Frustrated

I am trying to get information about life policies and all Nigel can say is that I have to go to the High Court twice and then the Houses of Parliament. I'm desperately fed up as I have to get my finances sorted out for future care. Nursing home fees are huge in spite of free nursing and personal care. I will probably end up selling the house. I have arranged visits to the Eastfield Care Home and two other homes.

20 FEBRUARY 2003

Visited Three Care Homes

In two days we have visited three different residential care homes, including the Eastfield. The Eastfield has much better surroundings, furnishings and facilities. I met a wife of a patient, who said her husband had been there for fourteen months and could not have been better cared for and he was very happy.

The other two homes were adequate but had rather small bedrooms and an awful lot of patients. I prefer the Eastfield.

They said they would give me a ring if a respite bed came up. Nigel liked the Eastfield but didn't enthuse about the whole issue.

24 FEBRUARY 2003

I found Nigel lying on the bedroom floor. He said he was defecating on the roof when he fell. I put him to bed.

27 FEBRUARY 2003

A Nightmare of Confusion

Nigel slid out of bed onto the floor at 5am. I attempted to pick him up. He said he was thinking about jokes and wouldn't stop talking about the "joke society". I tried to pick him up by rolling him onto all fours and prising him up. He was sodden - pad and pyjama top (he doesn't wear bottoms). While doing this, I felt a bit faint and lay on the floor. He told me to get a move on and get him up. I managed but had to attend to his needs - a urine bottle and complete change of pads. He went back to bed and slept. I felt a bit wonky but at 8am he said he wanted a bath, so I had to get up.

I think the time is just about ready for long term care. Every day is becoming a nightmare of confusion and I can't get out much without wondering what he's up to. He is really very frail now and needs help with every aspect of life. He didn't know who I was this morning. The whole day was awful and I kept having to watch what he was doing in case he hurt himself. He objected to my instructions and was very difficult.

49

1 MARCH 2003

A Distressing Lack of Companionship

Nigel is very confused most of the time and losing his way about the house. Eating is becoming difficult and a lot of the food lands on the floor. He is fairly mobile and can walk around the block. There is very little constructive interchange of conversation, partly due to deafness (his hearing aid isn't helpful) and mainly due to an increasing expressive dysphasia (and hallucinations).

Occasionally he can find a relevant document in the office but most things are left to me. There's a distressing lack of companionship, particularly as he's unsure of my identity. He thought I was Margaret Thatcher - too awful!

When I talk to him about long term respite care and the future, he switches off or talks about expense. I would like to look after him forever but his condition makes it difficult for me to be civil, with increasing weariness and his constant need for attention in every aspect of daily management. I foresee never getting out at all, unless I organise external agencies to come in, such as a sitter, which is not always easy and he may be resistant to this. Is there light at the end of the tunnel without long term care?

5 MARCH 2003

Sheena McNab Visits Again

Sheena McNab, the social worker, visited today. Nigel sits very quietly during these visits and only contributes actively when asked about his hallucinations which he likes to talk about. He has quite a lot of insight into the subject, although in other respects his reasoning powers are fast abandoning him. Sheena suggested day care and is looking into places. I think 9.30am-3pm is too long a session but it is geared to give me a chance to get out.

Also under consideration is respite care, where he goes to stay for a few days in a care home. A complete assessment of physical, mental and financial aspects was completed and the document signed by Nigel and myself.

6 MARCH 2003

Day Care

The psychiatric nurse has had the go ahead for Nigel to attend the Farringdon Day Clinic for day care activities and assessments. Dr Hammond is there to see him at intervals. It is a fairly long day and I don't know about Nigel's stamina. I declined having personal care assistants to dress and bath him at home as I thought it very intrusive so early but I may change my mind.

51

7 MARCH 2003

Life Is Pretty Horrific

Nigel was very difficult today and wouldn't get into the bath in a safe fashion and when I rebuked him, he promptly stood on my bunion which was excruciating. My language was unprintable. Eventually, his bath was completed but breakfast was difficult as he wanted to make a lot of toast to feed the parliamentary cabinet. Apparently, I have now become Prime Minister but I didn't get a bit of toast!

Life is pretty horrific and I can hardly sit down without being disturbed or, alternatively, having to find out what Nigel is up to while I am elsewhere in the house.

13 MARCH 2003

A Dreadful Happening

Nigel was fine at breakfast but later I found him with his underpants down having defecated on the sitting room floor - a huge amount of solid material. He was lying on his side and when I opened the door, he told me to get out. I did go in and did a massive cleaning up operation, taking his shoes outside to hose down as he had stood in the faeces and trampled them round the carpet. I also had to change all his clothes.

I find this behaviour quite unacceptable, even taking into account the dementia, and think the time has come for hospitalization. My sister-in-law, Marion, concurred with this when I phoned her in a distressed state. I also phoned the psychiatric nurse and left a message about the incident.

Nigel's response was that I had reacted unfavourably and he hadn't done anything out of the ordinary. I feel bad that I can't be more understanding, but he monopolises my whole life and there is precious little to enjoy these days. I also feel so sorry that I can't help him more emotionally.

14 MARCH 2003

I wrote to social worker, Sheena McNab, as I was unable to reach her on Friday as she had time off. I said in the letter that I would like long term respite care to be considered more acutely and described the recent problems. I also enclosed a copy of an admission form for the Eastfield Care Home, signed by Dr Green, in case it would be helpful.

16 MARCH 2003

Dementia Is So Unpredictable

Two very disturbed nights. Up at 3am and 6am with the apnoea machine, and trips to the loo with Nigel and nightwear changes. At breakfast, he wrapped his pill in a tissue and put it aside and was reluctant to take it. He never remembers to take his pill, although laid out in a special container with an "After Meal" notice on top.

Nigel is less sure of who I am and said yesterday that we ought to have a meeting to discuss my appointment and role in the house. He thinks we are in the army a lot of the time, harking back to his early army days. When he is quietly sitting in a chair, looking fairly benign, I can cope but once he is on the move I have to be wide awake to any new adventures. Dementia is so unpredictable; situations can change in minutes!

17 MARCH 2003

Nigel is going to the Farringdon Day Clinic tomorrow for day care, which is an over-65's unit for the professional assessment of dementia and other psychiatric conditions. There are key workers, occupational therapists and physiotherapists. Programmes are arranged for patients depending on their aptitudes. I hope he has the stamina as he spends so much time resting. I shall take him for 11am, as the bus which takes the patients spends a lot of time touring round collecting and he would have to be ready at 9.30am, which is very difficult.

21 MARCH 2003

Day Care at the Farringdon Clinic

I had a dreadful night with Nigel's hallucinations in the early hours about a red and white cat. Later, he got up and shed his pad in the bidet and got back to bed unprotected. I told him to "pad up" himself. I felt a bit worn out and drifted off to sleep and awoke to find Nigel had gone downstairs and eaten a plate of cornflakes. I didn't bath him but told him to have a good wash in the basin. The important result of this change in routine was that he had very little of the postural hypotension symptoms which usually accompany a full breakfast after a hot bath. I must alter the routine.

Nigel attended the Farringdon Day Clinic today and was welcomed by Cynthia, the senior nurse, who is Nigel's "key worker". She, with others, will care for him. She showed me all the facilities which include psychiatry, general medical check-ups, chiropody, bathing, occupational therapy and physiotherapy.

About twenty patients, mostly men, assembled for coffee and were then divided into groups for various activities to encourage interaction, mental stimulation and relaxation. Attendants cope with incontinence and other problems, and medication is handed out at the appropriate times. Nigel was quiet but enjoyed the company and three course meal and was quite happy to go three times a week.

The main problem is getting him there by 11am because that is the time of his worst post-eating and post-bathing postural hypotension, when he becomes completely switched off mentally and is unable to move about without lurching and staggering and going ashen. This can last for up to an hour and I have to propel him manually to the car for his journey to the clinic. Once there, he is able to get out of the car and walk.

If it weren't for this very difficult episode before the appointment, it would be a great relief for me to have some freedom. I've enjoyed the few hours to meet friends. In order to avoid the hypotension episodes, I tried getting Nigel up an hour earlier at 7am but that didn't make much difference.

26 MARCH 2003

The social worker has been in touch with the Eastfield Care Home and faxed the application. It may have a series of respites starting in April but there will be no certainty for a few days. Nigel is rather switched off on returning from day care at the Farringdon Day Clinic. They sent him home with wet trousers - another stripping and washing necessary.

28 MARCH 2003

Finally Some Respite Care

The social worker, Sheena McNab, has provisional respite care at St Augustus' Care Home for five days, starting on 5 April and coming home at the weekend.

4 APRIL 2003

Nigel went berserk in the bathroom and grabbed my wrist and nearly sprained it as he didn't want a bath, which he had asked for half an hour before. Fed up.

5 APRIL 2003

A Week's Respite at St Augustus' Care Home

Nigel was admitted today to St Augustus' Care Home for five days respite. The only room available was a pokey room with en-suite loo and basin, looking out at a brick wall.

He was anxious on admission and a bit demented but we had tea together and I put away all his belongings. Periodically, a carer would appear and introduce themself. One carer said the home was chronically short staffed and the carers underpaid - a cheerful thought for a new admission.

A carer took Nigel for a walk round the building and gardens, while I paid a cheque to a head nurse. I also had to hand over a Power of Attorney form which she was going to duplicate. What a fuss for a week's respite. The other residents were mostly at some stage of dementia and mostly too deaf to communicate.

6 APRIL 2003

I called in to the clinic the next morning with fruit and a Sunday Telegraph and found Nigel anxious, saying he had had a ghastly night because a power drill was breaking up concrete outside his window (not true). The nurse said he had had a "disturbed" night. Nigel was fussing about everything but told me to go and play my golf match, so I left and am preparing to do just that.

Nigel had no pads on, which I put right, and the en suite loo was cluttered with dirty pads and dribbles. He wasn't shaved and he said he had had a bath but I doubt it. There were no relevant staff around and when I later phoned, the nurse said she had been working on a different wing. I feel pretty awful as Nigel kept asking me for the keys to the house. John and Kate are anxious and both want to come to stay.

11 APRIL 2003

Back Home Again

Nigel is very disorientated since discharge from St Augustus'. On the day of discharge, the "matron" called me to say he had been quite compliant in behaviour until the day of discharge when he had refused point blank to have a bath, to have help with dressing or to go to the dining room for lunch. I packed up his things and brought him home with all he was dressed in - a pair of trousers, no underpants and a woolly jersey. Once home, I bathed him and washed his hair and washed a huge amount of clothing.

13 APRIL 2003

Our daughter, Kate, is staying with us and keeps Nigel cheerful but his behaviour has deteriorated and he is quite unable to understand instructions.

14 APRIL 2003

Worn Out

A bad night with Nigel stripping off pads and my having to wash a huge amount of soiled bedding. I gave him a ticking-off for removing a heavily soiled pad and shoving it into the midst of his bed clothes. At this, he just looked quite blankly at me and I realised yet again that I shouldn't waste my breath. It is so difficult caring for him now that I would welcome good long term care. I hope that won't be too far away, as I'm mentally and physically worn out.

21 APRIL 2003

Moments of Clarity Are Disappearing

Nigel's mental reasoning is declining very quickly and he has started making long, almost non-stop, rambling verbal excursions into new and obscure mental territory. He is also very difficult to manage, particularly in the mornings - refusing to take pills and clenching his teeth when given a pill in a teaspoon. Later on in the day, he has no recollection of earlier events.

John is home for the Easter weekend. Nigel is very pleased but spent most of the time sleeping in a chair, except for meals. He eats a lot and then feels rotten and nauseous and goes quite blank, unreceptive and unmanageable. The moments of clarity are fast disappearing and, although he responds to visitors, it is with an automatic social façade which belies his lack of awareness of the actual occasion. Finding out about financial investments and the whereabouts of documents is almost impossible. John is getting to grips with sorting out the muddle.

27 APRIL 2003

A Ghastly Dilemma

Nigel is so difficult, I'm hard pressed to cope. Last night at 3am, the apnoea control box crashed to the floor and I had to get up and disconnect various tubing and Nigel's face mask. I left it off, as I wanted to check it in the morning. As a result, he snored for spells and at other times was restless. He started wandering about but at last settled. He often knocks items off the bed table and occasionally the apnoea machine goes west.

Later at 8.15am, he took his clothes off and I decided I would have to get up and direct him to the bath. He tried to shut me into the bedroom as he said he had important activities on. I tried to lead him to the already run bath, whereupon he grabbed my two middle fingers and twisted them. Having arthritis in these fingers made for a painful experience. Eventually, he let go of my fingers, now very sore, and got into the bath talking absolute rubbish.

This is always a very bad time of day and I wonder whether there is any remedy for this particularly aggressive behaviour, which he forgets about by lunchtime. He is horrified if I mention his activities to him, which I do to explain my slightly distant behaviour to him. I am in a ghastly dilemma - whether to admit him to hospital on the grounds of these worrying aberrations, or whether to keep him here and cope.

He is more pleasant, although quite abnormal, during the later hours of the day. Although he is a monstrous burden, I feel I am enjoying the products of his enormously hard work to finance and build a happy home, although sometimes he is like a stranger.

30 APRIL 2003

Mad as a Hatter

Nigel got up at 4.45am, still attached to the apnoea control box which crashed to the floor, and I found him peeing into the waste paper basket. As he had a full pad on, it didn't go anywhere except on the pad. After breakfast he went to the lav and expelled noisy wind, saying to me that he was exercising his air conditioning system!

His hand wound has broken down. The circulation in both hands is so bad that the skin breaks down and bleeds, so I am dressing it with special dressings from the practice nurse.

2 MAY 2003

Alzheimer's Society

Nigel was so difficult this morning and is, I feel, physically deteriorating. He got up at about 7.45am and wanted a bath. I said I would get up and run it and he could get back to bed. He did and fell asleep and I could hardly move him to the bath. He has a real Parkinsonian gait now and he shuffled to the loo and performed on the floor. His bed was also wet through and I had to change it and turn the mattress. The mattress is protected by heavy blankets and plastic so the mattress is not wet, but needs turning to be aired.

After breakfast, at which he was quite turned off, he came upstairs and sat on the loo without taking down his underpants.

I had had enough and told him if he didn't behave, I wouldn't look after him. He said ok and that someone downstairs would do it. He kept trying to push me out of the bathroom and shut the door on me.

I got him to the Farringdon Day Clinic for day care and told the nurse he was being very difficult. On my way home from the Farringdon I called in, on impulse, to the local Alzheimer's Society office. They listened as I asked for advice on good care homes for the demented. They are not allowed to give recommendations of nursing homes but they were most kind and gave me a cup of coffee and reassured me that I was not being unreasonable about wanting a break. One of the advisers phoned up the Farringdon to make enquiries about respite, as she knew the senior nurse there, Cynthia (Nigel's key worker). Apparently, there was a possibility of respite and I would be phoned at home later.

Straight to Ward 12

There must have been a series of phone calls between various social work teams and I was told at 2.30pm that Nigel had been accepted for immediate respite care at Ward 12 of the Warwick Hospital, for five days, on recommendation of Dr Hammond, his psychiatrist. I was a bit nervous about Nigel's possible reactions and my friend, Linda, kindly agreed to help me carry his cases and apnoea appliance. Linda helps as an ex-occupational therapist volunteer at the canteen in the Warwick Hospital, a few yards from Ward 12 - Nigel's destination.

The ward is locked and only accessible to key medical staff. Once inside, Nigel was sat down on a chair beside a large TV which was blaring away amongst a motley crowd of patients, who all looked rather disturbed and ill at ease. Some had repetitive hand or body movements and one was lying on the floor writhing about.

The staff were very busy with files and telephone calls in a small office. I approached one and asked for some information about the purpose of the unit, other than respite. It is apparently a research and multidisciplinary unit for dementia allied mental illnesses. I was told about the meal routines and in turn told them about the apnoea machine and Nigel's pill dosage. Then I was shown his bed in a small four-bedded locked ward. His clothes were taken away to be marked.

Nigel wanted to know the purpose of the visit. I told him he had been chosen as a special and unusual case for studying and for the understanding of his rare condition. I know he wanted to come home but Linda told me to go out of the ward and she would chat to him and reassure him. I feel rather devastated that it has come to this but I have to accept that, if I am to retain any health or sanity, I need a break as I am gradually becoming very weighed down by running a one-woman nursing home.

3 MAY 2003

Angus, Marion and Linda have all visited Nigel, as they suggested I take some time off. They reported back that Nigel was aware of their presence but not really with it, and he talked about organising some army project.

I phoned the staff at Ward 12, who said he won't settle at night with his apnoea mask and has to have it monitored at night. Also, during the day he gives them long complex stories about obscure thoughts. I will collect him on Tuesday afternoon at 2.30pm. Heaven knows how I will cope.

The social worker, Sheena McNab, has arranged for a nurse to visit our home and assess Nigel's physical and mental state for care in the Eastfield Care Home. He will be put in the non-dementia wing if he is not too far gone for that, but there is a big waiting list.

6 MAY 2003

Home From Ward 12

I collected Nigel who was laying forth to the occupants of the day room about some committee meeting - he is very hallucinatory. He wasn't particularly pleased to see me and didn't seem very anxious to go home. On arrival at home, I found he hadn't a pad on and had wet the car seat and his clothes, so my first job was to clean up and do a wash of all his soiled hospital clothing.

Nigel talks all the time and is obsessed with some incident concerning the University from the distant past - something quite trivial but from which he can't divert his attention. It's very wearing. On the whole, he doesn't seem to have objected to his hospital stay although he was quite bewildered by the other occupants and the change in routine, and is unable to tell me much about any individual.

He has only been home for about three hours and already I am needing more respite. I feel pretty mouldy with stomach upsets and extreme fatigue. Cynthia, from the day centre, said they could take Nigel in every four weeks, for a week, if Nigel would agree to that. I would prefer to look after him myself but I doubt if I have the energy and mental stamina for it. I have been looking after him for seven plus years, including the last very intensive four years, and people vary in their ability to cope with stressful situations.

He is expected to go to the Farringdon Day Centre again tomorrow, if I can manage it. The night staff at Ward 12 said that he was very disturbed and had little sleep so I will see how he behaves at home in his own bed. I usually manage about four to five hours sleep per night and sleep through some of his activities, I think.

There is now very little about him that I can identify with my beloved husband. He is querulous and talks about himself all the time and hasn't any reasoning powers left - a terrible situation for him (and me).

Social worker, Sheena McNab, has left a message - she wants to talk about respite.

8 MAY 2003

Another Flood

Nigel had a long sleep but the bed was very wet. I took him to the bath and put his soiled pyjamas into the bidet and turned the tap on. I then rushed downstairs to do breakfast and came back up to find the bidet overflowing all over the floor. Then I heard a noise downstairs in the hall. The water had come through the ceiling and was cascading down the electric light wire. I rushed about with towels, buckets and mops and then Nigel had to be got out of the bath. On hearing of the situation, he said "It's a good opportunity for you to do some spring cleaning". That's all I needed! It turned out to be quite true, as I ventured into corners untouched for years!

Social worker, Sheena McNab, phoned. She is coming on Tuesday to discuss residential respite with the Eastfield nurse, Janet, who is also coming here to assess Nigel for respite. Janet phoned to hear of current events and says she is handing the case load to Cynthia and Sheena McNab. I asked Janet about Sinemet having hallucinatory side effects and whether there is an alternative. She will consult Dr Hammond. I will phone the incontinence nurse for thicker night pads.

11 MAY 2003

Incontinence Nightmare

Nigel is confused all day, talking rubbish and getting a bit suspicious about ordinary things. He thinks there are double meanings in actions and puts his finger to his lips in hushing mode.

Nights are bad and disturbed and he is very incontinent in spite of fluid reduction in the evening and thicker bed protectors. I have huge loads of washing to do and lots of incontinence pads to dispose of. Also, he goes to the loo and pees all over his underpants and onto the floor and then needs a clean change, although his trousers and underpants have only been on for an hour or so. I got so fed up with this in an unguarded moment, I told him he ought to do the decent thing and go into a home. I could visit him and take him out but wouldn't have to do all the nursing and cleansing chores. He didn't hear me which is a blessing as it is awful to blame someone for incontinence and dementia but I do give him very careful and repetitive instructions into how to avoid these accidents that are so time consuming. (It's a waste of time).

This morning at breakfast, I couldn't get to my usual seat as he had pushed the table about. When I requested entry, he said I should go elsewhere as it didn't suit him to move. I felt like clearing off forever! I will do lots of gardening and try to forget it amongst my flowers.

13 MAY 2003

The 13th is Living Up to Its Reputation

Nigel disturbed me for about the third time during the night to say the burglar alarm was activated with a warning signal. He was rushing back and forth. Although he can hardly move his limbs first thing, he was in full "athletic" form. I couldn't reassure him that everything was alright and eventually we got up. He was difficult in the bath and wanted to pee all the time. I also found he had peed on the floor beside his bed but he said it was someone else who had done it!

Last night we both went out to play bridge with friends. The game was very slow. We had coffee and some wine during the evening which may have contributed to Nigel's problems in the night.

Assessment for The Eastfield

Sheena McNab, the social worker, arrived at the house for Nigel's assessment for the Eastfield Care Home. Then a charge nurse arrived who worked in the downstairs dementia unit, and then a male "upstairs" nurse for the non-demented.

After about half an hour's chat about Nigel's abilities and daily habits, the male nurse said that Nigel would be, in his mind, quite suited to the non-dementia unit provided he wasn't inclined to wander. I asked if there was a chance of respite soon and he said the fact that they had been asked to come here for an assessment visit suggested that there was a place in the offing, possibly in a week or two

.

Nigel remained impassive and volunteered very little. He said he couldn't understand anything the male nurse said as he had such a strong Scottish accent. Afterwards, he said to Sheena McNab that he would understand more once he had learned the language. He thought the nurse was completely foreign!

18 MAY 2003

An Odd Episode At Supper

Nigel was ok for the first course and then decided he couldn't eat his pudding at the table because he needed a "left-handed homosexual ice cream to disarm some bombs!". Then he went into the kitchen and crawled on all fours pushing a three legged stool. He said he was keeping his head down to avoid bombs. During this operation, he set off his community alarm pendant and a phone call came asking if he had had an accident. He calmed down later but I'm disturbed by these ever-increasing episodes.

27 MAY 2003

It's Time For Long Term Care

I'm feeling very low and hardly have the energy to get up in the morning and face the awful tirade of rubbish, wet beds and laundry, with hardly a chance to go out and be normal.

John came for the weekend and was helpful and sorted out the garden and Claire, my daughter-in-law, came for a short spell which brightened the house up.

It's time for long term care. I have been weak enough to tell Nigel that I'm finding life tough and that care soon would be a help. He just looks blankly at me. He thinks he's no trouble and that I'm being churlish. The only way I can get peace is if I could sleep forever!

69

5 JUNE 2003

Another Disturbed Night

Nigel got up an hour early and I had to change his pads. I tripped over his walking stick, which he leaves in awkward places, and thought I had broken a bone but I'm ok. He has been very disturbed lately and keeps talking and making very odd notes in his poor writing, listing the different sequences of hallucinations which I think he had whilst in Ward 12.

I'm getting quite cross with him as he never does anything you think he might manage, such as shaving. Nothing happens unless you're standing there with the shaver to give to him. This morning he spat (accidentally) on the bathroom scales which was foul to clean up!

9 JUNE 2003

A Week's Respite at Ward 12

Nigel is in Ward 12 again at the Warwick Hospital for a week's respite. I need a rest. I have had a very busy week sorting out stray documents about benefits - Council Tax and Attendance Allowance. The council tax people lost all the forms sent for "Council Tax Relief for the Severely Mentally Handicapped" - a form provided by the psychiatric nurse which I didn't want Nigel to clap his eyes on.

When I visited Nigel in Ward 12, he was very disturbed and thought he was in charge of something and was reluctant to move from his seat. He kept hushing me as he was "getting" important information from the nursing station about the management of patients. I left quite soon after, as he wouldn't relate to me at all. I asked him if he had slept well and he shook his head and that was about all the feedback I got from him. I don't know how I'm going to cope with him after this respite as he is losing touch with his home way of life. After a week at home he is then going to the Eastfield.

17 JUNE 2003

Pulse 48

Nigel returned from Ward 12 and was like a zombie and unable to tell me about the routine. He was convinced that he was to attend a conference and thought I knew all about it.

His deafness makes communicating very difficult and his deaf-aid irritates him with awful background noise. His appetite is the only thing that's normal. The morning after his return, I had difficulty waking him (pulse 48) and so let him lie for an hour longer than usual but was keen to give him his Sinemet pill. This I did with huge difficulty after I had washed him all over and dressed him. I had to pull and haul at him to get any movement, and at one stage I thought of phoning the doctor and having him hospitalised. I persevered and eventually helped him downstairs where he managed some breakfast at about 10.30am.

As the day went on he was quite immobile and sleepy, except at meal times. Then after lunch he told me he was going out to a swimming pool and all sorts of other out of character suggestions.

18 JUNE 2003

I mentioned his dazed behaviour to the nurse at the Farringdon Day Clinic. She said that nearly all patients reacted in this fashion after respite. I wish someone had told me. Nigel had a very long sleep and got up and bathed today without problems.

21 JUNE 2003

Nigel Weighs Nearly 12 Stone (Up 5lbs)

Nigel was very disturbed after a long sleep. I got up at 6am to change his pads and then he slept until 9am.

I ran a bath but he wouldn't go to the bathroom as he said the bedroom windows must be closed in case some special dust blew in. I refused to go along with this and he was silent and grumpy and kept tapping his stick on the floor. When we got to the bathroom, he wouldn't let me pass through the door to organise the bath and pushed his full weight against me and pinned me to the radiator. I pushed him off and then he wouldn't get into the bath the safe way, so I tried to manoeuvre him into the right position whereupon he grabbed my wrist and twisted it - agony. I said I would divorce him if he didn't let go. My wrist is still sore and I was hoping to play in a golf match today. Sometimes I hate him, and now I don't feel so bad about putting him into respite.

23 JUNE 2003

The Eastfield Care Home

Nigel was admitted today for respite at the Eastfield Care Home for one week. He was given a beautiful room with en-suite loo and a shower with alarm pulls, and also an alarm pendant for round his neck. The carer nurse took lots of notes about his habits and dietary needs. Then a staff nurse checked on all the medical aspects of his care - all very thorough. It's a lovely clean place. I took Marion, my sister-in-law, for a visit on a subsequent occasion and she was very impressed.

Nigel is very hallucinatory and the new surroundings have confused him. Because he is not in the dementia unit, he has the freedom to climb up and down stairs which he likes to do at home to strengthen his legs. In the Eastfield this is considered unsafe and they were concerned by his very busy climbing. They solved this by putting him in a huge and comfy chair in the day room in the dementia wing with two other patients who were sitting quietly. He didn't seem put out and the next day he was back in his room lying on his bed. I think he's got the message and is not going about so much.

I am distressed by his incontinence and his inability to manage the mechanics of his incontinence pads. On two occasions he was very wet and I spent most of my visit stripping him. I told the nurses and they thanked me for changing him but they weren't concerned. I think the problem was that he had been fiddling with his pads and the nurses have a different system of care. The food is ok and he looks forward to meals and the staff are very friendly and the general atmosphere is good. Nigel is a bit lonely as none of the other patients communicate that much and are mostly wheelchair-bound. Although not demented, they seem a bit short of communication skills.

I don't know how I am going to cope when he comes home. I would be pleased if he could go into the Eastfield permanently, as I think they would make him comfortable when they get to know his ways. John and Kate visited Nigel and went for a short walk round the grounds. He chatted but again reverted to discussing his hallucinations.

30 JUNE 2003

Home Again

John and I went to collect Nigel from the Eastfield. He was sitting like a zombie with very little animation. I'm used to this, so I got him to his feet and walked him about a bit and gradually he emerged from his dream-like state and went to the car.

He settled down well at home after a few hours but kept worrying about his future programme. I told him I was going to London to visit John and Kate, and he would be staying for a week in Ward 12 again. He asked about dates so many times that I had to write them all down and he studied them for at least an hour. I hope I make it to London. Nigel has only been home a few hours and it's been constant input - taking him to the loo and helping to feed him which is now a difficulty. He says he hasn't had a bath for ages - not true I think. I wrote to the Eastfield to find out about the long term waiting list.

7 JULY 2003

I am still explaining to Nigel about my trip to London and his respite which Cynthia, his key worker, has now extended from 8th to 18th June. Nigel is anxious about everything and unable to use his reasoning powers, so constant reassurances and repetition of plans is necessary. He is also pretty obstructive to my plans, especially the suggestion of long term care. He says he feels quite fit and that we'll run out of money for my old age (if I have any!) As he is unaware of his mental shortcomings and of the behavioural problems and his bizarre and obstructive manner, he thinks I'm discarding him.

9-13 JULY 2003

A New Vision of Life

Away with my sister-in-law, Marion, visiting John, Kate and Claire in London and having a new vision of life.

14 JULY 2003

Back home from London and a visit to Nigel. He is being well cared for in Ward 12 but is disturbed, depressed, refusing pills and being a bit difficult to manage. His walking is erratic and the staff find that initiating movement is difficult. I can make him walk quite well but I know the techniques and am not put off by the "stop start" Parkinson's problems.

Nigel showed very little pleasure on seeing me and couldn't take on board much of my information about the family in London. He was annoyed that he wasn't coming home immediately and said that he must be consulted about the respite bookings. He threatened to take out a "habeus corpus" petition against my decisions. Not a pleasant interview. He also said that he notices a glint in my eyes that suggests I am hallucinating! How I'm going to manage, I can't imagine.

I had notification that a case review at the Farringdon Day Clinic on 25 July has been postponed until 18 August.

20 JULY 2003

Nigel is home again and managing quite well after the spell in Ward 12 which he thinks is some kind of ship. The staff are kind and considerate and there is a good standard of care. The Farringdon Day Clinic is also a very caring place.

22 JULY 2003

Sleeping Better

Nigel has been bothered by a chesty cough and chokes easily if coughing during meals. In terms of general mobility, he can walk 200 yards before resting and is able to stand from sitting and able to go to the lavatory, mostly unaided.

He is sleeping better and the apnoea appliance is fitting more comfortably and is less noisy. He tends to retire to a private world of hallucinations. It is difficult to interest him in current topics, although he does like to talk a lot about his delusions, trying to make valid interpretations of them. One subject seems to merge and become related to a totally unrelated subject and a complex and confusing solution results. Nigel tries to justify these solutions and no amount of alternative ideas offered by me is considered valid. It's easier for me to listen and nod occasionally than get involved in what turns into a "circular" argument that ends up where one started without achieving any progress.

24 JULY 2003

My Scrabble group arrived and Nigel greeted each one and then withdrew to lie down and rest, while we played. At coffee time, I went to collect him and when I went upstairs he had taken all his clothes off which made it tricky! I took him up a tray of goodies and he had them in bed and was very pleased. He is becoming quite childlike.

26 JULY 2003

Woken at 3am by high pitched yells - Nigel having a terrible nightmare.

28 JULY 2003

A Dreadful Morning

I woke up to find Nigel walking about with a strange assortment of clothes on, saying that he was going to the ski slope. He then went downstairs and set off the burglar alarm. I shot into action and told him he was too old to ski and then I ran his bath. I dressed rapidly. I took most of his clothes off, which were on top of his pyjamas, and when my back was turned he got into bed again. I tried to persuade him gently that a bath was a good idea but he said we both had to go skiing.

When I tried to help him out of bed, he grabbed my knees and stuck his nails in - quite sore and then he crunched up my fingers which was very painful. I had to lie down for a few minutes as I felt dizzy and tearful. I told him I could no longer look after him if he behaved like this, and he said that he always did everything I told him and now he wanted his own way. I said I only told him what to do to save him getting into a muddle. I hope long term care comes soon if this is to go on. I have a very busy day ahead with friends and family visiting.

31 JULY 2003

A bill came from the Eastfield which I paid by cheque. No word of placement.

1 AUGUST 2003

In A World of His Own

Nigel is very tired and sleeps a lot of the day. It was very difficult getting him ready for the Farringdon Day Clinic. I had to help with his walking - more so than usual. Cynthia from the clinic remarked on his uncharacteristic behaviour, detachment and refusal to comply. When he came home, he was more his usual self until he announced that he was in great discomfort about the scrotum. I pulled his underpants down and found that he had put a pair of spectacles and a separate spectacle case between his scrotum and his incontinence pad. I'm not surprised he was uncomfortable! He had no idea that he had put them there and I insisted that they should be suitably washed.

While I was out gardening, he had taken a lot of cushions off the chairs and left them lying around. He is living in a world of his own, detached from reality, although he occasionally has glimmers of reason. Cynthia has kindly managed to extend his next respite visit in Ward 12. She is very helpful and a credit to her profession.

2 AUGUST 2003

John and Claire arrived and Nigel responded well but got very tired towards the evening after some red wine. He and I had a very discordant time at bedtime when he just wouldn't get into bed and kept dithering around finding odds and ends to do. He is now unable to understand the simplest instructions, although this varies from day to day.

5 AUGUST 2003

The Disease is Galloping Along

I took Nigel to the bath today and en route I had a really sore cramping pain across my chest. It passed. It happens occasionally but I think it's stress and I don't want to fuss about it.

When we reached the bathroom, Nigel peed all over the floor and carpet so I had to forget about my chest pains and get on with it!

I went out to play Scrabble with friends and when I came home I found Nigel almost immobile in his chair and had great difficulty getting him upstairs to bed. I considered phoning for an ambulance as I thought there might be a major problem but I waited a bit and gradually got him to his feet and then to the stairs, which was a very laborious job. He was able to brush his teeth and wash his face and came to, as though out of a deep coma. A number of phone messages were scribbled illegibly on a pad by Nigel. Kate had been home to be with him but had gone out. I think the disease is galloping along and I fear the future.

6 AUGUST 2003

Apnoea Tubing Broken

Overnight, Nigel managed to dismantle his apnoea machine and distort the brand new tubing that arrived a few days ago (after a lot of negotiating with the clinic about posting it). All the careful reinforcements of one of the tube terminals was stretched and bent. I may be able to salvage it. I tried to put it temporarily in use at 4am but one is not at one's best at that hour! Fed up about that. More work needed.

8 AUGUST 2003

Feel Almost Bereaved

I had a very disturbed night with Nigel. He was extremely unsettled and the apnoea machine is a bit tiresome and noisy. I slept fitfully and then Nigel decided that he must have a bath at 7am which I gave him and I left for a short time to get myself dressed. When I returned, he was trying to climb out of the bath and was in a most precarious position and difficult to move.

I managed to get him to the lavatory because of his Senacot dose - no luck. I tried to get him off the loo and his legs buckled under him and I took the full weight, which was very uncomfortable. Eventually, I managed to dress him and get him to the breakfast table, where he managed to eat, but he felt dizzy afterwards and had to lie down.

He is very difficult to move about now as the Sinemet pills are losing their effectiveness. Kate helped me to get Nigel to the Farringdon Day Clinic.

At the Farringdon Clinic, I spoke of my problems and inability to cope and Cynthia arranged for Nigel's admission to the Raeburn Hospital later in the day. Cynthia and Kate accompanied me with Nigel to the Raeburn. Cynthia coped with the directions and administrative work. We met the ward nurse and care assistant and psychiatrist.

Nigel was a bit disturbed but we left him. He will remain at the Raeburn Hospital until his respite at Ward 12 of the Warwick Hospital on 18 August where he will be admitted, as I understand, for as long as it takes to find a nursing home (preferably the Eastfield). I feel shattered, almost bereaved - John and Kate are very sad too but I think it had to happen.

9 AUGUST 2003

Feeling Quite Lonely

Kate visited Nigel at the Raeburn Hospital, as I thought I might unsettle him and make him want to come home. Kate reported that he was quite "away with the fairies" and trying to give a lecture to the other patients about Russian consuls and was speaking more and more loudly to an amazed assembly of demented patients. The staff tried to get him interested in going for a walk with Kate but he refused point blank.

Kate came home soon as there was no communication and every time she tried to speak to him he hushed her and spoke even more loudly to the company. The staff said he had settled well, apart from this episode. I feel quite lonely and can't help wishing his admission hadn't been necessary or that I hadn't been instrumental in it.

11 AUGUST 2003

A Twinkle In His Eye

I visited Nigel with Kate and took him round the grounds in a wheelchair. He ate chocolates and was happy and talked all the time about some dreams or past experiences or hallucinations. He didn't ask to go home and seemed more settled.

One of the staff said Nigel had a good appetite but hadn't slept well because of his apnoea mask. They said he was no trouble and had a twinkle in his eye. He is very variable depending on the time of day. It is so sad to see him so changed, but the staff are caring well for him and he is well groomed and shaved.

18 AUGUST 2003

Long Term Residential Care

Today was Nigel's case review. Dr Hammond, Cynthia and Sheena McNab were present. We had a pleasant discussion about Nigel's condition and the speed at which the dementia is advancing, along with the failure of his autonomic system. The conclusion is that he needs hospital care and that I've managed long enough.

A bed has been offered again in Ward 12 of the Warwick Hospital, with a possible transfer to another ward until a space at the Eastfield becomes available. I am happy with this arrangement as I know he will have good care. Sheena McNab and I had tea at the canteen, while Nigel was being registered in by a doctor and student. I decided he had been through enough and I would visit him later in the week.

22 AUGUST 2003

Chocolate Cake

For the past few days, Kate and her friend have been visiting Nigel in Ward 12 and the highlight of these visits is going to the Veranda Café, next door to Nigel's ward, and producing a small box containing Kate's chocolate birthday cake. Nigel eats his slice with a spoon and it seems to transform him for a short time - all smiles.

After his cup of tea and cake, we go for a trip round the grounds in a borrowed wheelchair. This format has been repeated for several days with visits from John and Claire. The warm sunshine and air are a change from the overheated ward. His mental state is poor and he can contribute very little but when he does, we feel pleased out of all proportion.

I hope the Eastfield has a place soon but there seems to be a long waiting list and entry is dependent, unfortunately, on the obituary rate.

16 OCTOBER 2003

Ward Transfer

Nigel has been moved to another ward at the Warwick for a few weeks (Ward 7) which is more up-to-date and a mixed ward - ten men and ten women. There is a large day room and several smaller sitting areas and a private visitor's room with tea-making facilities and comfy chairs which is handy if the weather is poor. Normally, I take Nigel out round the grounds in his wheelchair and then to the Veranda Café for tea. I bring fruit and cake.

Nigel's behaviour is increasingly detached, dysphasic (receptive and expressive) and his thought processes very disturbed. I am still recognised and greeted in a friendly manner but there is always an element of anxiety in his demeanour. He is mainly preoccupied with "running the ward, university department and army barracks". His hallucinations add to these preoccupations and communicating with him is well-nigh impossible. He is also very deaf and his deaf aid is not helping.

I phoned the Eastfield about the waiting list - no joy. I also mentioned that they haven't paid me the social work refund on care received (personal care, nursing and medical). The assistant on the phone said she would try to trace the money and forward it.

Nigel will probably have to be reassessed for the Eastfield as his condition has deteriorated since his respite in June. Although he is well looked after at the Raeburn Hospital and is becoming aware of his surroundings, if his last years were spent in a well-appointed and peaceful environment like the Eastfield I would feel that the best was being done for him even if I have to sell the house to finance it. After all, all the possessions we have are due mainly to his very hard work and, as a good caring husband in the past, he deserves the best care.

2 DECEMBER 2003

Admission to the Eastfield Care Home

Nigel has at last been admitted to the Eastfield Care Home. A lovely en-suite room has been provided and visitor's access is free at any time. The staff are very helpful and kind to the patients and there is always a buzz of activity going on.

Nigel, not surprisingly, is overwhelmed by all the changes. Firstly going to the Raeburn Hospital in August, then to Ward 12, then to Ward 7, and now here.

Nigel's general demeanour is one of confusion and slight irritation and concern over financial matters (which he doesn't understand). It is a pity he can't appreciate the comforts more but the staff say it takes time to settle and so far his appetite has been very good. "He likes his food" said one auxiliary nurse!

Unfortunately, Nigel's watch went missing at the Warwick Hospital and also eight jerseys disappeared in the laundry. The ward have not been back to me about the missing watch and I may be able to reclaim some insurance. The watch was chosen by a Professor that Nigel used to work with as one of his parting presents when he retired from lecturing.

2004: THE EASTFIELD

JANUARY 2004

Settling Well

Nigel is settling quite well at the Eastfield and has a fairly comfortable routine. He is always clean and well cared for and the staff are very friendly and always willing to help. His general mobility is variable. The Parkinson's rigidity is more pronounced and the "stop start" problem is more evident. Some days he can get up and walk about and other days he needs two nurses to help.

His comprehension is limited and he has a marked vocabulary loss, probably expressive dysphasia, and I suspect receptive dysphasia also, not helped by poor hearing. I visit him almost every day, mainly in the afternoon, and we can all sit in his nice room or join the other patients in the very pleasant day room which always has a nurse on duty. The catering is very good and visitors are always offered tea and cake if it is an appropriate hour.

I have compiled a photograph album documenting his childhood, army days and friends, so that the staff can chat to him about the photos. I also added his interests in the past, such as bridge and golf. As well as this, there is a chapter from a book written by one of Nigel's army colleagues, giving accounts of a large number of their years in the Army, fifty years ago. I have written an account of Nigel's time as a university lecturer. The staff find this interesting and one staff nurse is making a study of this type of reminiscence aid as a help for communication.

Nigel still seems anxious and is often preoccupied with ideas that are difficult to follow. He is also constantly telling me he has a lot of lectures to prepare or exam papers to mark. I think the Eastfield is as good as any and I think he is settling. He doesn't ask to come home. He enjoyed a visit home with the family on Christmas Day but it took a lot of organising and I think summer outings in the warmth will be something to look forward to.

APRIL 2004

Nigel is gradually declining mentally and physically but is settling into a routine and eating well. I ordered a wheelchair (no free chair as he can't self-propel). He still recognises friends but is unable to sustain much social interchange. Poor soul.

A Nasty Fall

Nigel fell and cracked his pelvis. An x-ray showed curvature of the pubic ramus. He is now non-weight bearing, probably for good, and has to be transferred by a sling. He is very tired but is slowly improving. His leg muscles are very wasted and his quads look very shrunken. The staff are very caring and have put him in a large adjustable armchair on wheels. I can take him out in the sun but the chair is not easy to manoeuvre.

His general demeanour is one of mental torpor and he is generally retiring into a world of his own. He had an episode of attacking the nurse and smacking my hand but I think he was a bit fevered with a urinary tract infection and felt rotten. The care at the Eastfield continues to be excellent.

SEPTEMBER 2004

Permanently In A Wheelchair

Nigel has settled well into the home's routine. He is now agitated if I take him out into the garden in a wheelchair in case I stay too long and he won't be back in time for some event. Not that he knows what is going to happen but feels that he wants to fit in with his carers' duties. It is not as though he is particularly happy but he has always had a slightly anxious and agitated approach to work targets and this is translated into his now reduced lifestyle.

He still recognises me and some of his close friends but most of his chat is completely unintelligible. Physically, he is permanently in a wheelchair, or wheelable tilt armchair, and he has bouts of urinary infections, runny nose and gummed eyes. The general care is very good and he is always well turned out and enjoys eating apples, chocolate biscuits and a cuppa.

The patients in his Unit, nine men and one woman, are changing as there have been several deaths - mainly a blessing but this distresses the carers. I'm getting to grips with the financial side of things and am coping quite well. I have enough money to keep going but am reassured that the house value is increasing and I can always sell up, as the house is really too big for one person.

22 SEPTEMBER 2004

Nigel: A Poem Written in Three Minutes!

The Visit

Each day a different response
Sometimes a smile but mainly
Blank eyes staring into some vague chasm
A distorted memory, a bizarre image
What goes on in the wasted brain
Invaded by the wicked neural enemy?
Is it tea time? Not yet, Jim, Jack
Peter, Bill, George and Alice. Not yet
A huge glossy apple, seized with
Pleasure and put to lips. Open wider
And joyous crunching and memories
Of youth. Bright summer days
Of hide and seek, of scaling trees
And tossing apples, green, red, yellow
A second of escape

27 OCTOBER 2004

Mini Stroke

I visited Nigel, who was lying on his bed having had a possible mini-stroke or TIA (transient ischaemic attack). He had apparently been sitting on the loo when he slumped and then had a fit, with foam coming from his mouth and had "jerking" limbs according to the auxiliary nurse. He was very drowsy and hot when I arrived and would hardly respond to questions. I told him he was to rest after fainting and he seemed to take that on board. There was some distorted speech but then he lapsed into a semi-comatose state.

I stayed beside him for half an hour during which time I took his pulse (68) and tried to assess if he had lost any limb function. There was a marked weakness of his left elbow extensors but gradually both arms were able to move about. I left soon and the nurse said they would give the condition 24 hours and then reassess. Kate and I were considering going to London in two days to see John, Claire and the new baby (my first grandchild). I don't feel like going as I worry about Nigel so much.

Later, Kate visited Nigel (about two hours after my visit) and he was talking a lot - the usual incomprehensible stuff. When he smiled at her, he showed facial asymmetry.

NOVEMBER 2004

The New Baby

I didn't make it to London. However, Claire and John brought the new baby, George, to stay for a few days. We took George to see Nigel. He is a beautiful baby and I wondered how Nigel would respond. We put George (10 days old - 9lbs 4oz) into his arms and Nigel gently put his arm round him and held his hand. Nigel seemed to register the tiny helpless baby's vulnerability and smiled and made us all feel joyful. We impressed upon Nigel the fact that he was now a grandpa and I think he took it in. We were all so touched by his response to the baby.

2005-06: A SLOW DECLINE

JANUARY 2005

Nigel's health is failing. Some days he is so tired he can't respond and sits with his eyes closed. Occasionally he has a glimmer of what's going on, recognising immediately a visitor.

He is also, during wakeful periods, quite ill-tempered and can hit out if frustrated by an inability to make himself understood. He has difficulty finding the right words to express himself and with his deafness finds communication very tiresome.

He is being tested for a urinary tract infection as he is a bit feverish so perhaps he'll perk up, but I think the disease is progressing and taking its toll.

MARCH 2005

The Disease Advances

Daily visits are pretty depressing. Nigel is permanently in an adjustable arm chair, either sitting upright or reclining. If he tries to climb out of the chair, it is put into the reclining position for safety. This frustrates Nigel; it would frustrate anyone. If he manages to get off the chair, his balance is so bad that he inevitably falls.

His mental processes are in sharp decline and, although his vocal chords are fairly intact, his voice is faint and he is unable to sustain a conversation, tending to fade out half way through a sentence. Not much of what he says makes sense and there is the feeling of overriding anxiety in his outpourings. About eighty per cent of his demented colleagues are anxious - it seems to go with dementia.

On a sunny day, I wrapped him up and took him on a wheelchair trip round the grounds. I felt that a change of air might brighten him up, but I don't think it made much difference. He kept grabbing at railings and branches so it wasn't a smooth journey. Also, when you push a wheelchair from behind, the occupant is unable to see you and contact is lost.

John and Kate visited yesterday and tried to engage him in chat, but he was hallucinating and giving a lecture to some imaginary army colleagues. It is very sad altogether for all of us.

Physically, he has constant urinary tract infections, his hands are covered with bleeding sores because of circulatory problems, and his eyes water and are red and irritable and his mouth constantly discharges saliva from a drooping side. He still recognises me but visiting is very sad for both of us.

JULY 2005

Urinary Tract Infection

Nigel has another more severe urinary tract infection along with a new symptom characterised by sudden jerky movements of all limbs and limited control of hand movements. This new problem may be due to side effects from a drug to control his over-production of saliva (a Hyoscine patch).

Several weeks ago, Nigel had another TIA and he may have had another today. He is very keeled over to the left side and is incoherent and generally weak. I don't think the outlook is good. He is to have a new medical assessment to sort out his drug treatment. I think the Sinemet has lost its muscle relaxing powers.

MARCH 2006

Excellent Care

Nigel has been in the Eastfield Care Home for around two and a quarter years, in their excellent care. He is always well presented, shaved and has clean clothes. The best thing about going into the unit is the absence of smells of incontinence and the busy activity of cleaners.

Nigel's general health is poor, with advancing rigidity of his limbs. This is characterised by the "stop start" Parkinsonian movements - one moment he can't let go of a rail or arm of a chair and the next moment he relaxes and does a fairly "complex" operation such as blowing his nose or unwrapping a sweet.

Mentally, he may recognise me but I'm not too sure. I visit most days for varying periods and give him drinks of juice, chocolates, grapes and try to chat but his comprehension is nil and he talks rubbish in a quiet voice.

The staff feed him, or Kate and I do if we are there at the right time. He usually gobbles up everything. The sores on his hands have all healed very well. He is permanently chair bound, except for a little exercise with the physiotherapist. He enjoys the exercise classes before lunch.

I feel sad when I visit Nigel but he is so unlike the Nigel I used to know that it is more like visiting one of my elderly patients when I used to work in geriatrics.

AUGUST/SEPTEMBER 2006

On The Critical List

The doctor from the Eastfield phoned to say that Nigel had a serious chest condition and could either be cared for at the

Eastfield where he might last a few days, or go to hospital for treatment. I decided, with difficulty, to choose the hospital which hopefully would prolong his life and allow Kate, who is currently working abroad, to see him again.

I waited ages in the hospital, having gone with Nigel in the ambulance, and eventually he was admitted to the admissions unit. He has pneumonia and was put on a saline drip for antibiotics and put on a special mattress to help his bedsores. He is on the critical list.

The family arrived, including Kate, and were a great support. Nigel responded to drugs and was moved to a single room and given nourishment through a nasal tube, which he managed to pull out. The speech therapist tried him on jelly and sips of water to establish if the swallow reflex was intact and pronounced that supervised feeding could start. We were all pleased and Nigel's eyes opened and he was more alert to surroundings.

Nigel was discharged back to the Eastfield for "terminal" care, where his strength is increasing. He is dressed and in the day room and eating very well. I think he recognised me and enjoys, I think, a push round the gardens in the very good weather that we're having.

DECEMBER 2006

Good Days and Bad Days

One of the newer female patients thinks Nigel is her husband and takes exception to my attention to him. I said "He's mine!"

and wheeled him out of her clutches. She takes his pulse and tells me how ill he looks.

There is a certain amount of interchange between residents and it is not all amiable. Patients often go into the wrong bedrooms and settle there and it is very difficult shifting them. Some open drawers and help themselves to sweets - not so good for the diabetics.

There is very little change in lifestyle. Nigel is physically chair-bound, has a good appetite, occasional TIA's and urinary tract infections and is mentally confused and unable to say much.

He has good days when he smiles and has a few reactions to conversation, and bad days when he is quite switched off or belligerent. Occasionally he laughs and I feel so pleased to see my old friend again.

EPILOGUE

December 2006 was Eileen's final diary entry. Life continued in much the same vein for another year until 3 December 2007 when Nigel died peacefully in his sleep at the Eastfield Care Home, at the age of 77.

The years immediately following Nigel's death, presented further challenges for Eileen. She was diagnosed first with bowel cancer and then with breast cancer. Fortunately, the cancers were detected early and, being the resilient stoical and optimistic character that she is, she bounced back quickly after surgery and treatment. She is now in remission from both cancers.

Eileen leads a full, active and sociable life to this day. She still plays golf, bridge and Scrabble regularly with her friends and enjoys visits from her children and grandchildren.

* * *

Ingram Content Group UK Ltd.
Milton Keynes UK
UKHW020718180723
425342UK00014B/650